Why Me?

By Ashley M. Polidore

DORRANCE PUBLISHING CO
EST. 1920
PITTSBURGH, PENNSYLVANIA 15238

Dorrance Publishing Co
585 Alpha Drive
Suite 103
Pittsburgh, PA 15238
Visit our website at *www.dorrancebookstore.com*

ISBN: 979-8-8860-4375-4
eISBN: 979-8-8860-4468-3

Why Me?

"Introduction"

As you begin to read my story. I don't want you to think of me as someone famous. I want you to think of me as every other woman you come across in your daily lives. I'm a wife, mother, sister, and daughter just like you. Reading my story, you're going to learn that you're not the only woman in the world going through situations you are going through or have gone through.

Have you ever watched the news or read on social media of something so crazy happening in other people's lives? Have you ever watched a thriller movie that had you saying that couldn't have been me? I was one of those women that thought that. When my life events happened, I thought, how could this be happening to me? This isn't supposed to happen to me, and that's when I said to myself, why me? I hope that you'll enjoy my story and can also relate to some of my life events.

Chapter One:
First Life Event

Becoming A Mother

Never in a million years did I think I would become a mother. I remember as a teen always telling my parents I will never have kids. My dreams were to graduate high school, go to college, be single, ambitious, and to live in New York City. Unfortunately, things didn't go as planned. Don't get me wrong, I did graduate from high school. I even enrolled online for college in my mid-twenties but living in New York City didn't happen.

I became a mother at the age of twenty-one. Around that time, I was living with my boyfriend Lil' Sims in Franklin, Louisiana in one of his mother's rental homes. When I told my mother the news, she was so excited she was becoming a grandmother as well as my father and brothers. Being a first-time parent, you wonder and ask yourself, am I even good enough to become a mother?

While pregnant, I was working at Kmart and Dollar General. Lil' Sims was working as well to have things prepared for our child. When I was around six months, my mother and I discovered at my doctor appointment that my placental detached a little which made my baby lose weight from not getting enough nutrients as needed. So, I became high risk and was kept at Women and Children hospital in Lafayette, Louisiana. When alone in my room, I would cry because I finally understood the love a mother can have for her child. I decided to make a promise to myself that I will always love and protect my child until my last breath.

My daughter was born August 11, 2012. I was so thankful that we both made it. She had to stay in the NICU room for a month while I pumped my breast for milk to have sent to her. After my doctor gotten control of keeping my blood pressure normal, I was discharged from the hospital, but my daughter had to stay behind until she was ready. I stayed at my parents' home until my mother told me to go home and spend time with Lil' Sims because she could of tell he was missing me driving to my parents' home mostly every day. So, I decided to go, and he came to pick me up since I couldn't drive because I had stitches. I can't exactly remember which day things happened. Anyway, I remember it was like yesterday.

I was sitting in our bedroom watching tv while he was in the tub. His cellphone sounded off and I yelled, bae, your phone sounded off!" Now, I don't know if I misunderstood his response, but I thought he responded, "Don't touch my phone. "So, I got up to get his phone and when I looked in his text messages, I found out he slept with his ex-girlfriend while I was in the hospital with our child. Instantly, I felt sick to my stomach because I would never think he would cheat on me. I approached him about it while he was in the tub saying, "You slept with your ex-girlfriend while I was in the hospital." He didn't know how to respond so he didn't say anything.

Then I walked off and went sat on the bed in our bedroom and my mind started telling me to leave him and raise my baby on my own. He came into the room, and he said he didn't want to sleep with her that he was forced to because if he didn't, she was going to kill herself because she deals with depression and to just let it go. Now, I know it was a lie he was telling me, but I did let it go because I looked at my parents. They stuck together to raise my brothers and I so I thought why not stick together so our daughter can have both parents in her life?

So, I did what he asked. I let it go and didn't tell our parents about what he did. Down the line, our daughter was finally able to be discharged from the hospital. I was happy but also nervous because she was still small. My mother decided to stop working and started an in-home daycare just to watch her granddaughter while I worked back at Kmart. I decided to let Dollar General go so I could have time to spend with my daughter.

While working at Kmart, I noticed I wasn't getting enough hours to bring home enough income. So, I started filling out job applications online and one company hired me. I became a Cage Cashier at a casino. It was a guaranteed twelve-hour shift, so I ran for it, but later Lil' Sims got laid off, so I just picked up the slack. While he searched for employment, he scrapped items on side the road to sell it for cash while I continue working at the casino. I remember being so tired that some nights when we would have our daughter, I would fall asleep with her in my arms then Lil' Sims would take over so I can rest.

I also remember being so tired working twelve hours back-to-back that all I could do is sleep until it was time for me to get back up again for work. I would see the frustration on Lil' Sim's face because I was always sleeping and couldn't help him with our daughter. So he would pack her diaper bag and say he's going by his parents' home. As a mother, I felt bad because here I am working twelve hour shifts to have income coming in but didn't have time for her. Some nights I would get lonely at work working twelve-hour shifts, so I would call Lil' Sims from the office phone just to see what he would be doing. He was always with his homeboy hanging out at home.

One day on my day off my mind kept bugging me to check his phone record on his laptop. What did I find? A strange number he always dials when I would be away from home at work. I came to find out Lil' Sims would be on the chat line while I was at work. Of course, I confronted him about it, but he said his homeboy would use his phone which I know was bullshit because either it was both of y'all together or just Lil' Sims alone.

Now I know you're wondering, did I leave him? Well ladies, no, I didn't because he asked me to let it go so that's what I did, and he said our daughter needs both parents in her life. At the time, that's all I saw were my daughter needs, but as a woman I started to put myself last throughout the years and I forgot my worth. When you become a mother, you love your child so much that you would sacrifice to make sure they are okay. Down the line when I looked at myself in the mirror, I became bigger on loyalty than love. Lil' Sims wasn't a bad father or person, but he couldn't stay committed to me.

In 2013 by being so lazy and tired, I became pregnant by not keeping up taking my birth control pill on time. I'm saying to myself how are we supposed to support another baby when we are already struggling to take care of the one we have now? When I told my mother, she didn't have that excitement how she had when I first became pregnant. So, Lil' Sims and I had decided to have an abortion.

The day it happened, I made sure I was off from work, and I just laid in the bed while the abortion pill took its process.

Laying there I couldn't believe I was doing this, and tears started falling down my face. After my body went through the whole process, I asked my doctor if I could switch from the pill to the depo shot. I thought it would help but being so tired and stressed out every time I would go to work, a blood clot would come out. I never told my doctor how I was feeling only that I wanted to switch my birth control again because I would bleed. So, I switch from the depo shot to the patch and things got better.

Chapter Two:
Second Life Event

Upgrade

Lil' Sims finally found a job as an offshore worker, and I found a more fit and comfortable job so I could focus more on our daughter. Around that time, my mother started back working and Lil' Sim's mother had our daughter more. To me, things were still a struggle because we didn't fully move our daughter in with us while we were trying to get on our feet. While Lil' Sims would be away offshore, I would pretend like I'm a single mother just to get through the day.

Down the line, family feud started to kick in. Lil' Sims used to come and tell me that his family would say I'm controlling him and anything he would say to them from his own thoughts they would say it came from me. I was never controlling towards him. I would motivate him and make him stand up for himself because I wanted the best for him out of life.

A few months later, Lil' Sims came to me and said his mother was kicking us out because we were behind on rent. My heart dropped because I was shocked and confused. He said the other reason why was because we weren't keeping up with the yard and I looked puzzled because I know I cut grass when

Lil' Sims would be away offshore.

So, we decided to start looking around for apartments from Franklin to New Iberia. Unfortunately, rent was way higher than we were paying. We were paying only $300 and everything we found was $400 and above. So, while Lil' Sims went back offshore, I started thinking if I have to pay this much in rent I might as well buy a house.

Now at that time I didn't even have over $100 saved. We were living paycheck to paycheck. I went to Google about how to buy a home. I came across a program called USDA. I had no clue what I was doing but I still went for it. I filled out all the information the program asked for and when I clicked submit, it responded a representative would contact me soon. My phone started ringing and I'm saying to myself I can't do this. I was afraid, doubting myself that I couldn't do something big. I answered anyway and the representative went over all my information and told me how the program operates. She told me I was able to afford a home worth $60,000.

Now when she said it, I couldn't believe it, not until she sent the information to me by email. All I had to do was start looking around at different homes in my price range and move on from there. I told Lil' Sims what I was doing and the sound in his voice stated he didn't believe we would make it as well. Then he started saying how he wanted to add on to his mom's rental home and I'm like, "Why? It's not even ours." It came to the point where I started telling him he could stay if he wants but I'm leaving, I remember late nights on the laptop replying to emails and doing paperwork that the program needed from me.

I was so determined that I put a little stand by my bed with the laptop open just so when I wake up, I wouldn't miss an email. When I finally found the right home, Lil' Sims was offshore, but I was with my real estate agent and my mother. Now keep in mind I was facing my fears jumping off the cliff. It took a while to find a home and when I did it was the end of 2013, and we became homeowners in January 2014. The day I had to sign paperwork, I was at work, but I asked my boss if I could go five minutes away to sign the documents for the home.

While signing my documents, I wanted to put Lil' Sim's name on the paperwork as well. Like I said, I had a lot of loyalty for him, and he was the father of my child. My real estate agent advised me not to put his name on the documents because we weren't married and who knew what would happen in the future, so I took her advice. She was also impressed how I handled paperwork through the whole process and said I would be a good worker to join the team, but I wasn't comfortable becoming a real estate agent.

We finally moved from Franklin to New Iberia, which was awesome because my job was five minutes away. When I finally walked in the home alone after work, I just fell to my knees and cried saying, "Thank you Lord, I made it, I did it even when my fear had me doubting, I still didn't give up." So, I tell anyone to this day you don't need a lot of money to get a home but don't let fear stop you from what God has set for you. Sometimes you just got to jump for the things you want because the more you wait, the longer it will take and might never happen. About a week later or so my father, mother, uncles, aunts, and Lil' Sim's homeboy helped us move and unpack while I was at work.

That year. I also learned that your victories could cause emotions in others, some good and some bad. Don't get me wrong, I didn't mind people telling me how proud they were for me, but I didn't want to make others feels bad like I was above them. I started hearing rumors like I was spoon fed and if it wasn't for my parents, I wouldn't have a home or anything I had now.

It built up so much anger in me because they didn't know the truth. They thought just because I had both parents there that they did everything for me. I want people to understand that it's not up to their parents that determine your life, it's up to you to decide where you want to be in life. I've seen rich people that gave their kids anything they wanted but their kids end up on drugs or having a record of trouble. The life my parents have is their own life, and I'm my own individual creating mine.

Chapter Three:
Third Life Event

Stillbirth and Arrest

In 2016, I was pregnant again. Around that time, I was ready to add on to my family. I had a home big enough and Lil' Sims and I were both bringing in incomes. Our first born was going to school in Franklin where we moved from so Lil' Sim's mother let our daughter stay at her home during weekdays. Then suddenly things started to go wrong. Lil' Sims was unemployed again, but I still had my job, so I started to work at different store locations in Lafayette to earn extra income.

Some days I would be so exhausted because I had morning sickness and my feet would be swollen by the time my shift ended. Some days I would be frustrated because when I would make it home Lil' Sims would have company so I couldn't really rest how I wanted. I remember feeling so depressed that all I wanted to do was lay in bed and just stare at the sunlight shining through the window. One day, Lil' Sim's cousin Karma cooked a good meal but when I started to eat, I would feel pain in my stomach to where I couldn't finish the meal.

March seventh and eighth were the most painful days for the first time in my life. On March seventh, I remember Lil'

Sims and I leaving from his mother's home from spending time with our daughter. We made it home and I had to use the bathroom. As I'm sitting on the toilet about to stand, I felt water drop from me into the toilet. I'm saying to myself, "Oh my God, I'm going into labor," but something didn't feel right. I started feeling clots passing, and I yelled for Lil' Sims.

He came to the bathroom and asked what was wrong. I said, "I feel like I'm going into labor, but I think I'm bleeding." He told me to stand up a little so he can look and when he did, he said I need to get you to the hospital because the toilet was full of blood. When we made it to the hospital, pain and pressure started in my stomach. March eighth I was five months pregnant and gave birth to a stillborn baby boy. I remember feeling empty and blaming myself because I probably was overworking myself. I didn't want to be around anyone, and I didn't want to hear sorry for your loss. Returning our sons baby clothes to Toys R Us was emotional.

As I watched the cashier swipe each item that was bought for our son, my anxiety and emotions got higher and higher to where I couldn't breathe and started feeling dizzy. I told Lil' Sims that I was going outside because I couldn't take it. I just needed to breathe and try not to have a meltdown in public. I was also in college online so after my loss, I decided to put my focus into my work to get through my day. Two months later, I was back working and still attending school online. Lil' Sims was back working for a different company.

On May thirtieth and thirty-first, I was arrested and charged with cyberstalking. Now, I'm not a stalker, but I can tell you how I was charged with cyberstalking. A few days before May thirtieth, I was off laying in the living room doing schoolwork. Our daughter was on a family vacation with Lil' Sims's mother and sister with a few other relatives. We made sure our daughter had everything she needed to go on her vacation and gave her belongings to her grandmother.

Lil' Sim's sister texted me asking if I spoke to him and I responded, "No, he is at work." She said he had a lot of smart things to say because she had to buy shoes for our daughter. I said that we bought her shoes, and she responded, "No, y'all going to pay me my money back." So, staying humble I said okay, and I continued my schoolwork.

A few minutes later, Lil' Sims called me and asked if I spoke to his sister. I said, "Yes, she said that we have to pay her back for buying shoes for our daughter, but I know we bought her shoes." He responded saying they started arguing through texts and she called me, my mom, and his biological mom bitches. He told me to look in my text messages because he sent me screen shots. I read everything then something inside of me just had enough of always listening to Lil' Sims about letting things go.

I told her when they return just pack all our daughter's belongings because she is coming stay with us now. She called my phone and said you know I don't do this back and forward and if I want my child come get my fucking child then hung up on me. Instantly, my anger went off the charts because my child is with you in another state, and I had no clue what she would do to my child because of the issue of what's going on. I kept calling her phone back-to-back and she wouldn't answer so I went on social media and posted that I was going to beat her ass and one of the family members let her use their page to see what I posted, and she commented, saying continue to kiss ass like I always do, and I responded I was going to kill her.

I even texted her phone saying, "Let me know when you

get back in town because I've had enough of being silent, letting Lil' Sims family walk all over me." On May thirtieth, I told my mother what happened, and she was furious and decided to come with me to get my daughter. Lil' Sims wanted me to go to the police and ask them to come with us just in case something would happen. When we arrived, everyone was there except his sister. They put our daughter's belongings in a trash bag, so I really didn't have anything else to say.

I just wanted my daughter so I could go. Lil' Sim's mom was on the phone so when she hung up, she said, "So Lil' Sims, you called your sister a bitch?" He said, "No, I didn't, she called me one," and he started to show her all the text messages and when she read it, she got upset because not only me, my mother, Lil' Sims's biological mother were spoken of, but she read messages about herself as well and she said now she sees. The ex-sister-in-law that attended the family trip wanted to push the issue of getting me arrested even when I was trying to show her the truth.

When I looked up, I was being arrested for cyberstalking. They had enough of my actions to get me arrested. They used the text messages, the back-to-back phone calls when his sister didn't want to answer, and they used social media when I said I was going to kill her. The officers really didn't want to arrest me, but the ex-sister-in-law said she would go over their heads and report them.

The next thing I remember I was in handcuffs going to the police station. Was I scared? No. I just sat on the bed and looked at the wall feeling empty and full of rage. I kept asking, why me? I started doing flashbacks from when I got with Lil' Sims all the way until now and I realized I've been through hell mentally. I was bonded out a few hours later and had a restraining order against me saying I couldn't go around his sister, and I had court. I had a felony charge that could have had me in jail for two years.

When my first court date came, the district attorney and I had faced a judge in a room. He told the judge that I admitted to threatening the victim, which was true, but I had evidence that she came for me. I was given a new court date and all the information I had, I gave to the district attorney. While other cases were going on, he called me in the hallway, and he said he was going to get this thrown out because he read the information. He told me sometimes I must be careful on what words to use when I express myself because a person can use that against me, and he told me what to say in front the judge when it was my turn. From the look on the judge's face, he could tell I didn't belong there.

When I made it outside, I just smiled, held my head high, and said, "You wanted to destroy me and take everything away from me because I stood up for myself but in the end, I still won with the truth." After I made it through everything, I didn't even want to come back to Lil' Sims family and didn't want my daughter going there either. Unfortunately, he would still bring our daughter there to see his mom. It took me a while to forgive her about what happened. Lil' Sims would want me to come with him and I would always say no because I was at peace, and I didn't want to go around anyone that would disturb my peace. One day, he ended up talking me into going.

While sitting there, I felt anger just came back and I went sat outside. The energy I felt I couldn't stand it and I started questioning myself, why am I putting up with this shit? Why do I continue to stay knowing I'm not happy? Time passed by and in 2017, I was pregnant with my fourth child. I was still employed because I didn't lose my job and Lil' Sims was still employed with the same offshore company. I started asking him to find a land job because I told him it was putting too much on me from being pregnant, working, and taking care of our daughter. It was already enough that I was high risk.

I was having another boy and very excited because I was seven months and close to the deadline. The night of November thirteenth, I remember waking up with pressure in my stomach. I said, "Oh, my god! I'm going into labor and I'm home alone with our daughter sleeping in her bedroom." I called my mom saying I needed to get to the hospital then I started feeling strange and I knew something wasn't right. I wasn't bleeding but I started sweating and losing my breath.

I got out of the bed feeling myself about to faint, so I held my self against the wall trying to make it to the kitchen for some ice to cool myself down. I kept telling myself, "Come on, you got this," until I made it back to the living room to sit on the couch. I watched my daughter slept in her bed from the living room crying telling myself don't give up and to stay up, but I felt my eyes closing watching my daughter and I felt peace.

I don't know if I was dying but I remember feeling so much peace, but my mind kept making me think about my daughter, so I forced myself to stay up and laid on the couch until my mom arrived. I laid my hands on my stomach and I felt my baby died. That's something I never admitted to anyone that I felt my baby died. When I made it to the hospital, I still was fighting with pressure in my stomach and moments later the doctor came in and told me my baby didn't have a heartbeat. He stared me in my face looking for me to break down, but I couldn't cry.

I looked up at him and said, "Okay," and he responded,

"You don't have to be strong all the time." I said, "I know." Lil' Sims came home when they told him the news. On November fourteenth, I gave birth to my second stillborn baby boy. After I was discharged from the hospital. Lil' Sims and I went straight to the funeral home to set things up for our baby and went home. My mom was already there, and she had the blinds open so the sunlight would brighten up our home, but she didn't stay long. I started moving around like it was a normal day like nothing happened.

I was in the bedroom putting clothes on the hangers to hang in the closet then I started to feel hate, anger, and sadness. I had a hanger in my hand, and I started hitting the bed with the hanger. Every hit got harder and harder, and I started crying and I held my mouth because I started screaming. The next few days, Lil' Sims and I were barely communicating. He would stay in the bedroom on the game, and I would sit in the living room watching tv. Then when I looked up again, he was going back offshore.

Chapter Four:
Fourth Life Event

Wedding

September 29, 2018 was the day Lil' Sims and I got married. Now, getting married is every girl's dream. I've been with Lil' Sims since I was nineteen years old and I'm twenty-seven years old now. I thought man this is it. This is my happy ending despite of the babies we lost, the cheating, and family feud, we made it to always and forever. I was so excited to plan my wedding and have my family in it. Lil' Sims was still an offshore worker so him and I would communicate on video chat while my mother would take his place physically. Of course, weddings always bring drama, but I just basically flowed through it.

A few months before, around June, I told Lil 'Sims that I needed a break from planning the wedding because I was stressed. So, he decided to take me to New Orleans in July. It was fun just to get away from reality a little. I got to swim and just relax my mind. When August came, I was so ready to become a wife because I felt like I been doing wifey duties for years and now it was time to get my title. Then one-night, things took a turn. Lil' Sims and I were sitting on the bed playing his Play Station having fun and his cell phone sounded off.

It was from Facebook messenger. I reached for his phone, and it was a female, but I didn't pay it any mind. I just thought it was an offshore worker and I gave him his phone. It was the action he did that made me start wondering. When I gave his cell phone to him, he just looked at it and put his cell down. The next day, while I was driving home listening to music just out of no where my mind started bugging me about Lil' Sims reaction from last night.

So, I just decided to follow my mind and get into FBI mode to see what was going on. I went straight to his desktop because he had all access to my emails and social site, but I didn't have his. I got into his Facebook messenger and what I read between him and the female just made me not want to get married. They had been conversating the whole time while I was planning the wedding, even when we went to New Orleans for a break. It was the messages talking about under her clothes that pissed me off. I thought he was done with cheating on me both physical and verbal. I knew it was a sign from God not to get married.

The wedding was paid for so I couldn't get a refund and I didn't want to be embarrassed in front of family and friends. So, what you think I did? I went on and got married anyway because I didn't want to be embarrassed and I still had loyalty so my daughter could have both of her parents in her life. Now, like I said earlier in my story, he's not a bad guy he just didn't know how to be committed to me and only me.

We made a good couple for partnership but the love I had for him was gone. I want people to understand the mindset I was in back then. Yes, I had the material things, but I wasn't happy. I treated myself like I was his property because no matter how much he cheated, I never allowed another man to touch me or have a conversation with me until one night I got curious.

Chapter Five:
Fifth Life Event

Jumping Off the Porch

Here I am one year later in 2019. I'm still married and still with Lil' Sims. One night sitting in the living room watching Netflix, I was home alone since Lil' Sims was offshore, and our daughter was at her grandmother's house since I had to work for the weekend. I was always a house girl. I would work and go home. For some reason that night sitting down watching tv, my mind started saying what if I conversate with other men? Then I said to myself, I'm good I don't need to talk with other men.

Something in my mind kept saying it wouldn't hurt, look how many times Lil' Sims got caught and most likely is still doing it. So, I created a social media page on Tagged. When I created my page, I remember being so nervous that I put I'm not looking for anything serious just a few laughs to get me through my day on my bio. Now I'm going to be honest, I've been with Lil' Sims since I was nineteen years old, so back then was teen level.

This is adulthood now, so I was on some grown man level, and I had no clue how to start a conversation with a man. Let's just say I had no game. So, I finished creating my page and loaded a few pictures to see how it would go. A few moments later, notifications started sounding off like crazy. So, I decided to go look and read the messages in my inbox. Unfortunately, I didn't like how majority of them approached me, so I ignored them because it was about sex, and I wasn't looking for that. A week passed and one guy caught my attention.

His name was James from Pontiac, Michigan. He was a gentleman and in his early forties. James and I would message everyday just to talk about how our day was going and make each other laugh. I told him I was married and how I ended up on this social website. He said some married couples are still together because of their kids but the whole time they are feeling miserable but sacrificing their happiness to keep a family together. Around the end of September, James and I had to stop conversating because he said he had a girlfriend and she started noticing how different he would be around her and showing her less attention.

He did admit he was into me and when he would lay with his girlfriend, he would imagine it was me. So, I told him we had to let each other be because at the end of the day, we could never be together. Then as days passed by, I would see him get online and the last thing I saw him post was, "I don't know why I continue to get on here," then his profile was gone.

October came in and that's when the unexpected started to happen. It was the beginning of the month and around that time our store is always busy. It was late afternoon, and around then we had less customers, so I was talking to my coworkers about James when a guy walked in the store. Now I've been employed with my company for a few years so seeing a man walk in the store was nothing to me and besides I never look at them directly in their face. My eyes were always more focused in my computer.

So, he came to my window and asked to purchase one of our store cards. So, like any other customer I started handling business. While attending to his needs, he asked if I remembered him. I looked at him and responded you do look familiar like I've seen you back when I was a teenager and I started focusing back into my computer. He said, "My name is Black." I said, "I remember your face but not your name." So, just like any other customer, I finished his transaction and told him to have a good day.

Later when I was done with all my paperwork, I decided to log on to my Instagram account to see what people have been posting. So, as I scroll, Black's picture came up on the timeline and I said to myself I never knew we were Instagram friends and I commented on his picture saying now I know who you are. After my long day of work, I went home, bathed, fixed something to eat, and watched movies until 1:00 A.M.. My cell phone sounded off and it was a notification from tagged. So of course, I went look and when I saw it was Black, I was shocked because first I saw his face at my job, then Instagram, and now Tagged.

So, his message said, "You remember me?" I responded, "Yes, I do, but were you searching for me? He said no that my profile just popped up in the area where he is from. He asked what I was looking for on here. I just said nothing but conversation because I am bored sometimes, and I'm married. He said he was married, too, but separated a while back and he asked if I ever stepped out on my husband before. I told him no I never did no matter how many times he cheated. Then Black asked, would you?

At that moment I got curious, but I didn't want to admit to it. Later after work, my cousin Christoina and I would drink wine, have our girl talks, and watch a movie. I told her about Black, and she said to remember you are married now. I responded that I know but look at everything what Lil' Sims put me through. Christonia sipped her glass of wine like, okay, I'm just telling you. I can admit in the back of my mind I know she was telling me the right thing but another part of me wanted to see how it feels to be touched by another man. I was nervous as hell because I've never cheated nor let another man touch me in over ten years.

Before it happened, I decided to make some rules for him and me, but one of them was for him not to fall in love with me. When it happened, I felt different and not different in a bad way. It was exciting and now I finally understood how Lil' Sims felt doing what he does. Black asked if I was okay and how did I feel. I said different. As days turn into weeks, the more we talked over the phone and messaged each other we didn't even realize we were falling for each other. Black made the flame that was burned out in me come back to life and I started realizing my worth. Black touched me mentally and physically.

When I looked up, I started putting me first, getting my hair done, nails done, wearing makeup, and cute outfits. I finally found me again, for once, I started worrying about my own happiness. The funny thing about cheating is the more you connect, the more emotions get involved. Don't get me wrong. I tried to stop. I even fell on my knees crying to God asking him to help me stop. I couldn't ask God for forgiveness until I knew it was over.

When you find that great feeling again, it's hard to let go. Down the line, Lil 'Sims found out about my affair because he had access to my emails to change the password to any of my social sites and my phone was under his name. To be honest, I thought it was my way out to finally leave Lil' Sims but he told me to stop connecting to Black or he was going to expose our messages on social media. I didn't want that to happen, so I explained to Black that I had to stop connecting with him. He didn't take it so well because he knew I didn't want to be with Lil' Sims anymore and from the messages Lil' Sims read, he knew how Black and I felt for each other.

Lil' Sims told me he feels like this was his karma because he knew one day, I was going to cheat but he never thought I would go through with it. I learned that people come into your life for a reason. I used to question myself, why did I cheat after all these years? All those guys through the years that tried to make their move and I ignored them, but it took this guy for me to get curious. Black and I still stayed connected as time passed by, but I faced my fears to tell Lil' Sims that I wasn't in love with him anymore and all I wanted was partnership for our daughter.

He did try to make me change my mind by taking me places and buying me things. It did make me happy at that moment but at the end of the day my mind was locked in on what I wanted for myself. I wanted to be happy on the inside as well on the outside. Lil' Sims and I had a talk and he asked me if he can have another chance and I told him I love him and care for him always, but I couldn't see myself falling back in love with him. So, when I gave him my answer, he stood up, gave me a hug, and said he was going to Texas, and that easily, he just left. I said to myself, damn, I stayed all these years through all the cheating and family feud, and he left just like that. That taught me to never put myself last for a man and to never give a man that many chances ever again.

Chapter Six:

Sixth Life Event

Dating Process

After Lil 'Sims and I separated, I decided to be alone and celibate to give some time for myself. I can't lie, just to be alone and have space was peaceful and relaxing. I would work, come home, bathe, fix a glass of wine, and watch a movie on Netflix or if our daughter was home, we would watch a family movie. I would converse with other guys on social media but never attempted to meet them in person.

Down the line when I did decide to start physically meeting men in person, I learned that this generation is very fast and advances more than how things use to be. The very first guy I decided to start spending time with was named Chucky. Chucky and I talked for weeks before seeing each other in person. So, one day we agreed to watch a movie together at my home. He went and bought food for us to eat while we watched a movie.

Things were going smooth between us, but you know sometimes you can look in a person's eyes and feel their energy. I can tell he was fighting a lot of demons from his past life. As weeks passed, I started seeing a side of him that made me fear him. He would get mad fast, yell and disrespect me, even threaten to beat me. So, I decided to ghost him and to get out the safest way possible.

After that, I was good, back to relaxing and at peace. I'm a person that prays a lot so I would have the blessed oil, sage, and candles just to pray for my surroundings and family. The next guy I crossed paths with was named JT. I met JT one day because my cousin in law was by my home and he came to stop by to pick up some shoes he wanted to buy. I was sitting in my living room and when he entered my home I said damn and hey.

He responded saying hey and went talk to my cousin in law. So, the three of us were sitting down in the living room talking about our past relationships. Later that night my cousin, cousin in law, and I decided to go out to a club. JT ended up coming because it was his birthday. I can admit I was having a good time because I had never been to a club before. I enjoyed the old school music they were playing, and I was enjoying the apple martinis. I went stood outside for some fresh air and JT was already outside smoking a cigarette. So, we started talking about our last relationships and how we didn't want to rush into another relationship because we went through so much hell.

When it was time to go, he asked if I wanted to ride with him going home since we were all going back to my home to wine down anyway. I agreed so I went grabbed my cellphone charger from the girls and told them I was riding with JT. It was nice riding, but I felt a little nervous then he held my hand while driving and I started to feel okay. He stopped by the gas station before we got to my home asking if I wanted anything from out of the store and I said no. We finally made it back to my place and my cousin fixed some food and went home.

My cousin in law was enjoying her time with her friend,

so JT and I sat in the living room and played music cuddling. Now ladies, you know how they say about one-night stands. Let's just say your girl had her first one-night stand and Lord it was good. He was prepared because he had protection, but I figure that was the reason why he stopped to the gas station.

After we were done, we started talking to my cousin in law and her friend then she said, "Y'all hear a horn blowing like crazy?" It was JT's ex-girlfriend; she found his car, so he went to look out the window saying, "Man, look at this girl, I'm about to call the police because she has been following me." So, he called the police to report her because he didn't want to go outside and put his hands on her then he would have been going to jail.

He waited a few moments then he left. Now I didn't give JT my number and I didn't contact him for a few days because I said to myself it was just a one-night stand. One day after work, my cousin in law told me that JT been asking about me almost every day and she even told him to contact me, but he was nervous. So, I asked her, "Do you think I should message him on Facebook?" She responded, "Go with your move."

So, I decided to message him so we could contact each other. Down the line, he would start coming by the house after work and we would give each other massages while talking about our day at work. JT and I lasted with each other from October to January. He ended up going back to his ex-girlfriend. Down the line, I tried dating a few more guys but it came to the point I just gave up and decided to throw in the towel. I had enough of the friends with benefits, the ones that acted like I was the only one, even the ones that wanted women to take care of them. June 2021 was the moment my life was about to change, and I didn't even see it coming.

I was working alone that day and a customer walked in

asking if he could cash his money order. Like always, never looking in a customer's face, I grabbed his money order and I.D. When I read his name, I looked up and said, "Mal." Mal was a very old friend of mine from teen times, but we lost communication. I said, "Boy, I didn't know it was you, how you been?" He smiled and responded, "I've been good, "and I finished his transaction and let him go on with his day.

As days passed, I started noticing he started returning to the store a lot wanting to cash money orders. It was so much until I told him he might as well get a job here since he's always coming. In the back of my mind, I started wondering if he was only making money orders just to see me, but I said I was just overthinking. He found me on Facebook one day and messaged me asking how I been then he would try to ask me out. Now, I saw he had a girlfriend so I said no because if she's a good girl, don't mess that up, I wouldn't even let him cross that line. He kept saying he was not happy, the things they put on social media are just for show. I kept denying him until mid-July. He called me through messenger one night while I was relaxing after work.

He said he was just checking on me and saying, "Damn, you're beautiful." I said thank you and he said give me a chance to be with you. I said, "Mal, you have a woman, and you know as a friend I would never let you cross that line." He said, "I'm a single man me and her are not together anymore." I said, "Yeah right Mal," and he said, "I'm serious." At that moment you know how your mind first tells you to do something, but you don't listen? Looking back that day I regret after all his trying I finally gave him the opportunity to conversate with me because he said he was finally single. So, we started video chatting throughout the day and night.

After I would clock off from work, he would come by the house, and we would just laugh joking around, and watching movies. I enjoyed being with him. I felt like I finally found a real male friend. It was the beginning of August, and we were still conversating, but I started questioning him about the vehicle he drove, and he told me his ex-girlfriend let him use it because she knew when she didn't have anything, he always had her saying she shows loyalty even though she know he talks with someone else.

Now I'm a woman. No woman would never let a man drive her vehicle unless they are together. We got into our first argument, and I said this was why I don't want to drop my walls and let you in because I'm tired getting hurt by men and I told him to leave me alone. It was next morning, and my feelings were still hurt while I was getting ready for work. Mal texted begging to come see me before I went to work, so I agreed since he wanted to explain himself.

When he arrived, I opened my door and I let him in, but we stood by the door. He started saying, "I apologize love, I apologize," and I was so hurt because I started having flashbacks of all the hurt I've been through with a man to where I just broke down crying in front of him and he wrapped his arms around me and held me close. He said, "What's wrong? Talk to me." I couldn't even respond because I couldn't stop crying. He wiped my tears and told me he was going to let me finish getting ready for work, and he was going to call later. Around the end of August, I caught Covid with pneumonia, so I really wasn't talking to Mal that much.

After I made it through Covid and the pneumonia, Mal and I started hanging out again. When we finally got together one night, he told me he was sick as well and that his birthday had passed. So, we were drinking and catching up but that night I can tell he was ready and so was I. He kept looking at me licking his lips like I was a hot meal and kept rubbing me on my thigh. He was a gentleman about it because he waited on me to make a move first. So, I jumped on top of him and as soon as I jumped on top of him, he grabbed me close and made love to me like no man had ever before.

The next day, I felt so different inside and out. I couldn't stop smiling remembering every detail of that night. I finally let my walls down and let him in. A few weeks later, I invited him to attend a family circus with my daughter and I, but I can tell something was on his mind. A few days later I was thinking of him, so I decided to go to his Facebook page because we weren't Facebook friends and what my eyes saw made my heart dropped.

There he was, the man I kept denying. The man that was constantly chasing after me, making money orders just to get a reason to see me. The man who told me he been tracking me for years knowing the jobs I had…married. The time when I was sick in August was the time he got married which means I made love to a married man because we met back up after I had covid. My heart dropped. I couldn't believe the shit I was seeing. I felt sick to my stomach because I felt like I broke up a happy home.

I told my cousin Christonia, and she was pissed off as well. I told her I don't want anything to do with him anymore. Later that night, Mal texted my phone and automatically I blew him down saying hell no! Go back to your fake marriage and leave me alone you are dead to me. He never replied and when I woke up the next morning to go in my Facebook messenger, I noticed he change his picture to him and his wife, which was supposed to be the ex-girlfriend.

I just deleted him out my messenger so I wouldn't have to look at his face. About three days later, he started calling me early morning through Facebook messenger. I opened the message and left him on read. Then he started calling my cellphone back-to-back. I never answered. Then he started texting my phone saying we need to talk please let me explain. So, I replied to his text saying alright. He called again so I went in the kitchen to fix me a cup of coffee and answered his phone call. He said, "Love, look I can't do this anymore."

He said, "I really didn't want to get married she planned the whole thing by herself and as I was getting dressed my mind fell on you." He started crying on the phone. I said, "Why didn't you tell me that you got married because if I would have known I would have never let us lay with each other because that night was special."

All my emotions came back, and I started crying. He said, I wanted to tell you, but I didn't know how you were going to react." I said, "Now you know. We can never be how we were, its too late and all we can be is friends nothing more because you are married now." Mal said, "I can't just be your friend and you are married yourself." I said, "Yes, I'm married but my husband and I are separated staying in a different state. We don't stay in the same household."

September came and he would still call or text but nothing further than that. Sometimes we would get in arguments because he would feel some type of way because I would be conversating with someone else. One day he called me all excited, saying he found a job but needed a ride to go do his physical. Now in the back of my mind, I'm like where is your wife? She can't take you? I am a good-hearted person and want the best for everyone, so I agreed to bring him to do his physical. A few days later, he was working and texted me saying thank you, you don't know how special you are to me and that I have a good heart.

In mid-September, he started asking if he would pay me rent to stay in the guest room, would I let him? At first, I was saying to myself no because it wouldn't feel right but then again, I could use the extra cash to save on the side. I asked why he wanted to leave, and he said because I don't want to be with her because she is a gambler and he had to get rid of mostly everything he had to get them back right. At the end of September, he was staying in the guest room paying rent. When I think about all this now, let's just say a predator knows how to hunt after its prey. In October things started to take a turn. I don't know if he was confused on what he wanted to do or who he wanted to be with.

One day, I even told him if deep down he thinks him and his wife still have a chance, I don't mind him staying in the guest room until things cool down and he can go back home and work on their marriage. Instantly, he got mad saying why would I say something like that, but I thought I was telling him the right thing. Then I said well, if you don't want my opinion don't talk to me about your wife. That was the first time I ever saw a different side of him.

He started disrespecting me by calling me out my name and I couldn't believe it like where is all this coming from? Later, he apologized saying he would never call me out my name again. Down the line, things got worse to where he started from mental abuse going slowly into physical abuse. Most nights, he would leave and not return until seven the next morning.

I couldn't believe I was going through this. He would never show his evil side to my daughter because he loved kids.

I tried to leave him, but he wouldn't let me go, saying I'm for him. One day he even went into my wallet and took some cash without asking and when I confronted him, he said to get the fuck out his face. I walked away saying fuck you and went to get in my jeep. He came running outside grabbing on my door, but my doors were locked, and he punched in my window.

Never in my life have I been in a domestic violence relationship. As days passed by, I tried not to make him angry, so I just started praying how I used to with the candles, sage, and blessed oil. Every day I would pray, asking God to remove anyone in my life that doesn't belong. November was my way out. He got arrested and I found out he was robbing people in my vehicle while I slept at night and he was on heroin. He was close to destroying my life because I could have lost everything but all I had was the truth and God on my side.

Chapter Seven:
Phoenix Bird Reborn

After everything was over and I was free from Mal, I was fighting depression. I kept replaying everything I went through with him. I decided to go to counseling because I wasn't strong enough to handle my emotions on my own. My very first day of counseling, I couldn't even say a full sentence without crying. My counselor said my life is never going to be the same but he does know I want to move on and get my life back. It took me three months to get myself back to normal. After I finished counseling, I was back but not the same.

I hated all men, and I thought every man had something to hide like they were living a double life. My counselor told me not to be so hard on the next guy but I wouldn't even allow myself to let a man get close to me. In a way, I felt like Mal still had me cage because he always said I belong to him and now I wasn't allowing any man to get close to me.

I became a bitter woman and didn't want to feel love. No one in my family knew what I went through, and I never wanted to talk about it. Some days I would have flash backs or memories that made me sick to my stomach. A month later, my cousin Christoina and her male friend tried to play match maker. I wasn't having it because I completely gave up on love.

I was so rude to this guy they were trying to get me to speak to that I called him a whore.

Fortunately, I didn't scare him off and now let's just say, he and I are like the Tyler Perry movie, "Diary of a Mad Black Woman." I thought the old me was dead and gone but I was re-born and came out stronger than anything. One night him and I were watching a movie about a woman who always wanted to be a writer and I said that's what I wanted to do. He looked at me and said, "Go write; what are you waiting for?" So, I automatically knew what I wanted to do. I wanted to tell my story to let other women around the world know they are not alone.

I want women to not feel embarrassed about what they went through in life. I want women to know you are human and you are not always going to make good choices but to always keep your head up high and walk like the Queen you are. Is your life going to be like a fairy tale? No, it's not, but we have the option to be better than we were a year before. To any woman that feels like you're not safe with a lover, my advice is to never panic and stay as calm as possible and when you see a clear path to run, you better run and never look back. As for me, I'm living life now and I'm better than the person I was a year ago.

God bless us all.

The End

www.ingramcontent.com/pod-product-compliance
Lightning Source LLC
Chambersburg PA
CBHW051337150726
47997CB00004B/1499